A Mediated and Partial Zone

ISBN 978-1-913749-32-3

Published by
GUILLEMOT PRESS
Cornwall
Printed and Bound by Palace Printers, Lostwithiel

A Mediated and Partial Zone

Betsy Porritt

GUILL EMOT PRESS

ENCOUNTERS

light a candle as evening falls
domestic and unavoidable, who are you
in relationship to this space?   Passenger
the law is made visible in certain paternal
rings   spectacular resistance
touching a relic that blessed 'clean' governance

footpaths invent themselves cannot be trodden out
waterruns over a shallow depression in the
public square, different alphabets lap lap lap   my
mum and I talk about my sister's eggs
I push at the scrim with my eyes closed
my nephews are tactile and puppyish

with my back to the core I'm looking out
a truck vibrates by to Dover
silences are blocked passages in our gut
intelligence   I keep on taking my shoes off
in private
we hear our neighbours, sound sutures us

I plant bulbs because I'm in love
with the closeness of promises   somewhere my
mother turns her attention to logistics
        we drink coffee from a flask in the crown of a
fallen Ash   I won't write the difficulty of being
numerous my hands are framing the daily

        between feast days and tax returns are concrete
blocks paving slabs iron sheeting and a weapon pit
                            a baby is crying in a
different part of this building
        I'm talking about acts of horticultural and civic
care

        I've made a triangle with my fingers tenderly
trying to enclose what I mean
                        holding you all at arm's length
        I can come in the time it takes you to clean
your teeth   turning my face to the ground so I can
bear witness to the future

EQUIVALENT MATERIALS

hours ooze contains 'we' and 'was'
now we threshold diagonally   eave deaf peeping
cottony holding place   we're bookshelf people
shoulder part of the building envelope
hold   pronounced 'house'

echo no *no* no *no*   come hold mine
name   a turned tied
  testing time   can only opt in
  turned hand linked to pocket
        homely or holy or homily

weeping   length of wood
pliant willow casket   pint accomplice
pinup trial   the worst of
both non-porous worlds
brick shock refusing   minor outrage

broke   what belongs
                     speak friend crack apart the sea
                          strip ready, soft bough
               sticky municipal finger
                          your fluorescent leap

arcade skinned rabbit aloft said
maybe a public chair   thin sunslip for
                    seeds borne on sticky flypaper
dragged blinking   somehow shared
particles feather   our ice flows

indistinct length   thin lip connector   rivet
golden marble eyeball   splinter
gobstopper whisperer   readdressing
the ground
blinking pin drop   rootling strip stump

delightful eyelid liquidity   russet dyed
strip to origin   plain metal body
rabbit eyes in the rabbit light
shared outline
          'your' safety is important to 'us'

seeking safer passage   grub grown
slivers   level against your plinth
      decomposition   hold
fast   roundel
transgressive orgasm   dug down groan

room crux   interleaving tones   scrunched
dime tissue secret rood passage
                    slim pliant length
cuddle   picturewindow   ululate
cupped around   juicy orange lungs

evil mouth box   pretty little wreaths
silent keeper draught excluder
      laugh   dowdy mistress hider
       struggled via an equivalent
dove through the wicked window

locker-room talk
white wiped tiles
ha ha ha
indistinct outline
rejoice empire dissenter

little imposter
lingering
at the window
raptor
doorway witness

exhibit on a sliding scale   rackety
pretty street boundary
face a white plastic bag   craw stuck
mere market meat   terror
                    vibratory coin edge

slough white wave ruffs   slap   slap   moan
          treble the knots on the sliding rope
       fly beat disturbance
       changing face of tender
       troubled wager   re-re-returning

deft turning
toward outer galaxy
soaring and ruining   clouds and roots
            gold against wallstreet
mourning   low yielding   crops

ear a small bridge   sliding pitch thatch
        held wheat and street dirt
    wreathed in fear
            dog bites   micro-roots
handshake

neither linen   thinner niche
slow kitchen   explosions
different metals   sing
silent bread histories
could be a place of spinning or root making

unlucky hand
shackles bite down on slim ankles
a gift going both ways
different metals between paychecks
words and laws   and locks   do that

blinking gorgeous
      metallic desire in the mouth
   pretty little gift
dove through the mirror
   struck off the back teeth

achey bathroom basket
avocado apricot peach pits
pearled   songbird
        wipe damp tiles
submerged mouth stones

donor rind renewed
          molluscs on ice chips   liquid against
whatever   saline mountain   pearling
          seeds borne on a fleshy bed
               germinate with me

mapped mountain   cold cold coin edge
borne on the high wind
secret wheat futures
different metals between handshakes
feels weird and bad

how to shoulder the   teeth futures

making eye contact   hands in continual motion

speak boney truth

    buckle under it's ok

        readdress the ground

dried at tide turn
picking tippety tip taps
chagrined at a molecular level
invisible contact with the roadway
contract to a pinprick   waiting

black seeds borne on hot air
thunderclap handshake
facing inward or out   palm taps on
sandstone slabs   high notes
scything through thick air

seeking shells we come up with washers
gutters between crop rows   whole
moon   turned fat and waxy
mind how you plate your dish
we know 'harvest' means dominion

shells all crusted over   buttery tasting promises
     dead metals between
     sworn enemies
       still biting into slim dates
     feared and thrived   at handfast

        pliant waterrun   pillowy and kind
rare equivalent to hours
collared on a long walk   sucking motion
        webs as networks as out of date maps
        condense into milky opals

always always partial
　　　　now moving out toward another globe
map a daily lengthening　　a fish and chip supper
　　　　　steps into lemony sunlight
　　　　here I am

for now little bread biter
we're wild grass people
waiting on the rushcutters
grubbied council vans   hold the tar rate
baked in a bottomless pie   and ate it

GUILLEMOT PRESS